SIR LEW GRADE and MARTIN STARGER present
A JIM HENSON PRODUCTION
"THE MUPPET MOVIE"*
Executive Producer MARTIN STARGER
• Produced by JIM HENSON
Written by JERRY JUHL & JACK BURNS
• Directed by JAMES FRAWLEY
Music & Lyrics by PAUL WILLIAMS and KENNY ASCHER
Co-Produced by DAVID LAZER
Starring The Muppet Performers JIM HENSON • FRANK OZ
JERRY NELSON • RICHARD HUNT • DAVID GOELZ
Co-starring CHARLES DURNING and AUSTIN PENDLETON

MUSIC AND LYRICS BY PAUL WILLIAMS AND KENNY ASCHER
EXCEPT *AMERICA* TRADITIONAL ARRANGED BY IAN FREEBAIRN-SMITH
EXCEPT *ANIMAL...COME BACK ANIMAL* BY PAUL WILLIAMS

Cover illustration by Michael K. Frith

Original Soundtrack   Available on Atlantic Records and tapes.

Look for the MUPPET MOVIE BOOK
A Muppet Press Book from Peacock Press/Bantam Books
©1979 Henson Associates, Inc.

*THE MUPPET MOVIE and MUPPET character names
are trademarks of Henson Associates, Inc.

ISBN 0-89524-061-0

Design: Ian Summers and Sally Bass

Concept: Jerry Houle

Piano Arrangements: Jack Perricone

The MUPPET MOVIE

CONTENTS

WORLD WIDE
STUDIOS

ANNOUNCE
OPEN AUDITIONS
FOR FROGS
WISHING TO BECOME
RICH & FAMOUS

2 P.M.
HOLLYWOOD
CALIFORNIA

THE RAINBOW CONNECTION

by: Paul Williams and Kenny Ascher

Why are there so many songs about rainbows,
And what's on the other side?
Rainbows are visions, but only illusions,
And rainbows have nothing to hide.

So we've been told, and some choose to believe it;
I know they're wrong; wait and see.
Someday we'll find it, the rainbow connection;
The lovers, the dreamers, and me.

Who said that ev'ry wish would be heard and answered
when wished on the morning star?
Somebody thought of that, and someone believed it;
Look what it's done so far.

What's so amazing that keeps us star-gazing
And what do we think we might see?
Someday we'll find it, the rainbow connection;
The lovers, the dreamers, and me.

All of us under it's spell;
We know that it's probably magic.

Have you been half asleep and have you heard voices?
I've heard them calling my name.
Is this the sweet sound that calls the young sailors?
The voice might be one and the same.

I've heard it too many times to ignore it.
It's something that I'm s'posed to be.
Someday we'll find it, the rainbow connection;
The lovers, the dreamers, and me.

La-la-la......

THE RAINBOW CONNECTION

Lyrics and Music by Paul Williams and Kenny Ascher

Moderately, with a lilt

Why are there so man - y songs a - bout
Who said that ev - 'ry wish would be heard and

rain - bows, and what's on the oth - er
an - swered and when wished on the morn - ing

side? ___
star? ___

Rain - bows are
Some - bod - y

12

14

MOVIN' RIGHT ALONG

Lyrics and Music by Paul Williams and Kenny Ascher

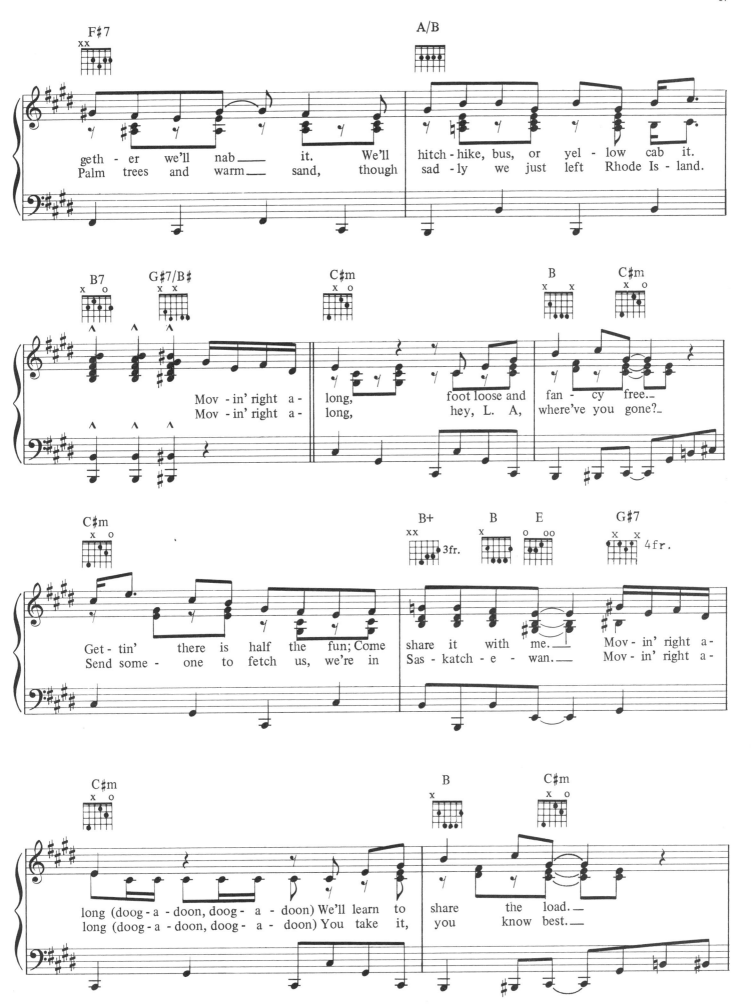

18

19

MOVIN' RIGHT ALONG

by: Paul Williams and Kenny Ascher

Movin' right along in search of good times and good news,
With good friends, you can't lose,
This could become a habit.
Opportunity just knocked, let's reach out and grab it,
Together we'll nab it.
We'll hitch-hike, bus, or yellow cab it.

Movin' right along, foot-loose and fancy free.
Gettin' there is half the fun; come share it with me.
Movin' right along (doog-a-doon, doog-a-doon)
We'll learn to share the load.
We don't need a map to keep this show on the road.

Movin' right along we found a life on the highway,
And your way is my way, so trust my navigation.
California, here we come; that pie-in-the-sky land.
Palm trees and warm sand, though sadly we just left Rhode Island.

Movin' right along, hey, L.A., where've you gone?
Send someone to fetch us, we're in Saskatchewan.
Movin' right along (doog-a-doon, doog-a-doon)
You take it, you know best.
Hey, I've never seen the sun come up in the West.

Movin' right along, we're truly birds of a feather,
We're in this together and you know where you're goin'.
Movie stars with flashy cars and life with the top down.
We're stormin' the big town.
Yeah! Storm is right, should it be snowin'?

Movin' right along, do I see signs of men?
Yeah, "welcome" on the same post that says "come back again".
Movin' right along, foot-loose and fancy free.
You're ready for the big time, is it ready for me?

Movin' right along
Movin' right along

(repeat to fade)

NEVER BEFORE, NEVER AGAIN

Lyrics and Music by Paul Williams and Kenny Ascher

NEVER BEFORE, NEVER AGAIN

by: Paul Williams and Kenny Ascher

Never before have two souls joined so freely, and so fast.
For me this is the first time, and the last.
Is this an angel's wish for men?
Never before and never again.
And where to find the words to sing it's worth,
This love was bound for heaven, not for earth.
This love was meant to light the stars,
But when we touched, we made it ours.
And would they take it back?

Oh, no, they wouldn't dare!
Why should they take it back,
When there's enough to share with all the world,
And fill the heavens above
With left-over love?

Never before, a love that just keeps growing on and on,
To fill each lover's heart and light the dawn.
Is this an angel's wish for men?
Never before and never again
Never before and never again.

28

I HOPE THAT SOMETHIN' BETTER COMES ALONG

Lyrics and Music by Paul Williams and Kenny Ascher

31

★ KERMIT THE FROG ★ FOZZIE BEAR ★

SCOOTER ★

FLOYD ★

SWEETUMS ★

STATLER ★

WALDORF ★

★ DR. BUNSEN HONEYDEW ★ DR. TEETH ★

MISS PIGGY ★ GONZO ★ CAMILLA ★ ZOOT ★ CRAZY HARRY ★

I HOPE THAT SOMETHIN' BETTER COMES ALONG

by: Paul Williams and Kenny Ascher

Can't live with 'em, you can't live without 'em
There's somethin' irresistabullish about 'em.
We grin and bear it 'cause the nights are long,
I hope that somethin' better comes along.

It's no good complainin' and pointless to holler,
If she's a beauty she'll get under your collar.
She made a monkey out of old King Kong,
I hope that somethin' better comes along.

Ah, but, what could be better than a saucy Irish setter
When puppy love comes on strong?
Or a collie that's classy, a laddie needs a lassie,
A lover and wife gives you a new leash on life.

I don't mean to scare ya, my friend, but I betcha
Come "Father's Day", the litter bug's gonna getcha;
The urge is righteous, but the face is wrong,
I hope that somethin' better comes along.

Still, it's fun when they're fetching,
And agree to see an etching
That you keep at your lily pad.
There is no solution, it's part of evolution,
You'll soon hear the souls,
The little feet of tadpoles.

There's no limitation to mixin' and matchin'
Some get an itchin' for a critter they've been scratchin'.
A skunk was badgered, the results were strong,
I hope that somethin' better,
I hope that somethin' better,
I hope that somethin' better comes along
Oh yeah!

AR-GA-Raga-ORK!

**"I JUST GOTTA CATCH UP
WITH THOSE GUYS!"**

Gonzo

Rowlf

Kermit the Frog

Floyd

Miss Piggy xx

Zoot

Fozzie

ANIMAL

Dr. Teeth

CAN YOU PICTURE THAT?

Lyrics and Music by Paul Williams and Kenny Ascher

An-y-bod-y's lov-er, ev-'ry-bod-y's broth-er, I wan-na be your life-time friend.
Let me take your pic-ture, add it to the mix-ture, there it is, I got-cha now.

Cra-zy as a rock-et, noth-in' in my pock-et, I keep it at the rain-bow's end. I
Real-ly noth-in' to it, an-y-one can do it. It's eas-y and we all know how.

44

CAN YOU PICTURE THAT?

by: Paul Williams and Kenny Ascher

Anybody's lover, ev'rybody's brother,
I wanna be your lifetime friend.
Crazy as a rocket, nothin' in my pocket,
I keep it at the rainbow's end.
I never think of money; I think of milk and honey,
Grinnin' like a cheshire cat.
I focus on the pleasure, something I can treasure.
Can you picture that?

Let me take your picture, add it to the mixture,
There it is, I gotcha now!
Really nothin' to it, anyone can do it,
It's easy and we all know how.
Now begins the changin' mental re-arrangin'
Nothin's really where it's at.
Now the Eiffel Tower is holdin' up a flower.
Can you picture that?!

Fact is, there's nothin' out there you can't do.
Yeah, even Santa Claus believes in you.
Beat down the walls,
Begin, believe, behold, begat.
Be a better drummer; be an up-an-comer
Can you picture that?!

All of use are winnin', pickin' and a-grinnin'
Lordy, but I love to jam!
Jelly belly gigglin', dancin' and a-wigglin',
Honey, that's the way I am.
Lost my heart in Texas, Northern Lights affect us.
I keep it underneath my hat.
Aurora Borealis shinin' down on Dallas,
I give it to a Texas cat.
Can you picture that?!

You got to see it in your mind.
Can you picture?
You know it's quick and easy to find.
Can you picture?
You don't have to buy a frame.
Can you picture? Can you picture that?!
Can you picture that?!
Use it if you need it; don't forget to feed it;
Can you picture that?!

KERMIT THE FROG ★ FOZZIE BEAR ★

SCOOTER ★

★FLOYD

★SWEETUMS

★STATLER

★WALDORF

MISS PIGGY ★ GONZO ★ CAMILLA ★ ZOOT ★ CRAZY HARRY ★

★ DR. BUNSEN HONEYDEW ★ DR. TEETH ★

I'M GOING TO GO BACK THERE SOMEDAY

by: *Paul Williams and Kenny Ascher*

This looks familiar, vaguely familiar
Almost unreal, yet, it's too soon to feel
Yet, close to my soul, and yet, so far away.
I'm going to go back there someday.

Sun rises, night falls; sometimes the sky calls.
Is that a song there, and do I belong there?
I've never been there but I know the way.
I'm going to go back there someday.

Come and go with me; it's more fun to share.
We'll both be completely at home in mid-air.
We're flyin', not walkin', on featherless wings.
We can hold on to love like invisible strings.

There's not a word yet, for old friends who've just met;
Part heaven, part space, or have I found my place?
You can just visit, but I plan to stay.
I'm going to go back there someday.
I'm going to go back there someday.

I'M GOING TO GO BACK THERE SOMEDAY

Lyrics and Music by Paul Williams and Kenny Ascher

51

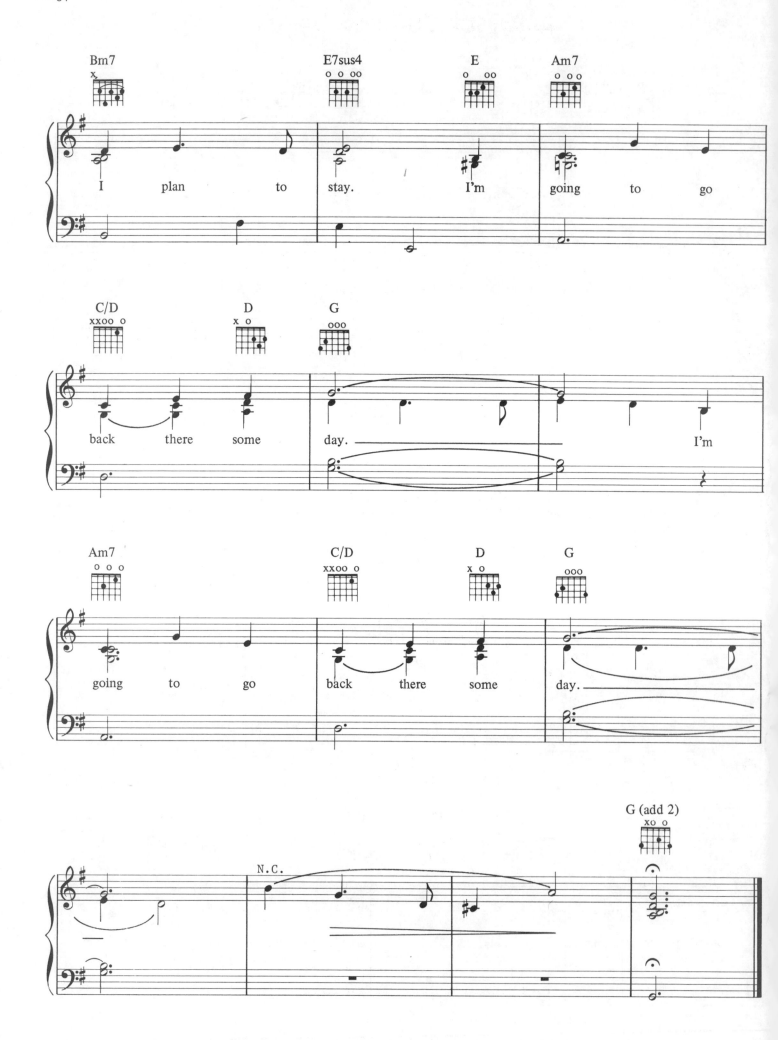

America the Beautiful

Traditional, arranged by Ian Freebairn-Smith

ANIMAL... COME BACK ANIMAL

by Paul Williams

Light Rock

F

cresc. _

B♭

Easy Dixieland Feel

THE MAGIC STORE

Lyrics and Music by Paul Williams and Kenny Ascher

Border (clockwise from top): KERMIT THE FROG ★ FOZZIE BEAR ★ MISS PIGGY ★ GONZO ★ CAMILLA ★ ZOOT ★ CRAZY HARRY ★ DR. TEETH ★ DR. BUNSEN HONEYDEW ★ WALDORF ★ STATLER ★ SWEETUMS ★ FLOYD ★ SCOOTER

THE MAGIC STORE

by: Paul Williams and Kenny Ascher

It starts when we're kids, a show-off in school;
Makin' faces at friends, you're a clown and a fool.
Doin' prat-falls and bird-calls and bad imitations;
Ignoring your homework, now that's dedication.
You work to the mirror, you're getting standing ovations.
You're burning with hope, you're building up steam.
What was once juvenilish is grown-up and stylish,
You're close to your dream.
Then somebody out there loves you,
Stands up and hollers for more;
You found a home at the Magic Store.

The Rainbow Connection (reprise)

Why are there so many songs about rainbows?
That's part of what rainbows do.
Rainbows are memories, sweet dream reminders
What is it you'd like to do?
All of us watching, and wishing we'd find it;
I've noticed, you're watching too.
Someday you'll find it, the rainbow connection,
The lovers, the dreamers, and you.

Life's like a movie, write your own ending
Keep believing, keep pretending
We've done just what we set out to do.
Thanks to the lovers, the dreamers, and you.
